PORTFOLIO 10

METROPOLITAN SEMINARS IN ART

Portfolio 10 · *Techniques*

by John Canaday

CHIEF OF THE DIVISION OF EDUCATION

THE PHILADELPHIA MUSEUM OF ART

THE METROPOLITAN MUSEUM OF ART

TECHNIQUES

Water Color, Pastel, and Prints

BY DEFINITION water color is pigment with any one of several water-soluble gums used as a binder. It is a convenient technique, requiring no more accessory equipment than a brush, a piece of paper, and a cup of water. It is also easy to clean up. For these reasons all of us meet water color in our first paintbox and continue to think of it as a technique for beginners. Actually, the proper manipulation of water color demands great dexterity and a sound command of the general principles of picturemaking.

It is usual also to think of water color as a slight technique, limited to charming, delicate, and inconsequential effects. It need not be so; we have already seen John Marin's *Singer Building* (Plate 29, Portfolio 3), a water color that can hold its own, for strength and brilliance and expressive power, against strong competition in any technique. There does come a point, and *The Singer Building* may represent it, where water color meets boundaries beyond which it cannot go. It is essentially an intimate technique; it cannot approach the grandeur of fresco (its first cousin, but compatible with the grand scale as water color is not), nor can it approach the sense of permanence of tempera or oil, nor oil's wide versatility. But water color should never be dismissed as trifling.

In its simplest application, as in a child's coloring book, water color is an adjunct to drawing, serving to fill in with the desired tints various areas where form and formal relationships are already determined by a complete drawing. This is true in Albrecht Dürer's *Madonna and Child with a Multitude of Animals* (Plate 109), a great pen drawing from the first years of the sixteenth century but not, properly speaking, a water color. The delicately tinted washes are entirely dependent upon the drawing for their meaning. As an addition to the elaborate composition they are charming, but they add nothing much in the way of explanation or enlargement, nor of course is that the intention.

Water color came late into its own. It was not until the middle of the nineteenth century that it began to emerge as a technique with its own potential for expression. Samuel Palmer's *View of Tivoli* (Plate 110), painted about 1838, stands somewhere between the use of water color as we have just seen it in the Dürer and its final independence. The color reproduction of *View of Tivoli* is reduced to about two thirds the size of the original; the black-and-white detail from the lower right is approximately full size (*Figure 1*).

View of Tivoli was a nearly complete drawing before any color was applied to it, and the preliminary pencil skeleton remains everywhere visible. Some trees at the extreme right foreground were roughly indicated to extend up beyond the horizon, but they were colored only in their lower portions, probably because the artist changed his mind as to their effectiveness in the composition. The rendering of details is quite meticulous, even into the ex-

5

treme distance, sometimes depending on pencil drawing, sometimes on direct painting with a brushtip fine enough to use like a pencil. But here and there the brush begins to come into its own, as in the highest patch of cloud to the left of center, where several tints—blues, grays, and a dull rose—have been allowed to run into one another in a way that capitalizes on water color as water as well as color. According to one school of thought this is the only real water-color passage in the whole picture.

The rays of light striking from the horizon up into the sky behind the hills have been created either by washing out the color in those areas or by erasing it. Although either method is possible in water color, neither is considered quite legitimate by purists. Finally, the picture was completed with a general touching up with gouache. The addition of a heavy white to water color makes it opaque; it becomes "gouache," with which most of us are familiar in the form of poster color. Applied thickly enough gouache will conceal other colors, no matter how dark they are; used in various degrees of dilution it will allow background colors to show through if that is what the painter wants.

Gouache is chalky, whereas water color is brilliantly transparent. The difference in texture is difficult to capture in a reproduction but is noticeable enough in various highlights and accents here. Gouache is used in *View of Tivoli* for the sprays of light foliage at the extreme lower edge just to the right of center; they are painted quite thickly to conceal the strong background colors. These sprays appear not to have been drawn in but to have been added as an afterthought. Their lightness accentuates the gathering dusk in the valleys. There the waterfalls have been struck in with a thinner gouache that still half reveals the forms beneath, as a thin fall of water would do. But the most conspicuous gouache passage is that of the large waterfall to the right, where the paint ranges from a thick, completely opaque white through all degrees of transparency.

Again, a purist would have preferred to see the white areas left unpainted, allowing the paper to tell. But Palmer was not interested in giving a demonstration of his dexterity in water-color technique; his waterfall is essentially drawn rather than painted. The closest approach to an accurate classification of this picture as technique would be "drawing: pencil, water color, and gouache."

Water color's special character as a technique interesting in itself lies in its fluidity and transparency. Neither of these characteristics was made much of in the excellent picture we have just seen. But in Winslow Homer's *Sloop, Bermuda* (Plate 111) these inherent qualities are fully realized.

Here the preliminary drawing is limited to a few cursory pencil strokes, a bare minimum giving a broad indication of the picture's arrangement and leaving the forms to be described as well as tinted by the pigment. The effect is very "wet"; the very feel of the flowing brush is still present. The texture of the paper, which is a part of this effect, is revealed in two ways. In some areas, as in the sky, the pigment has been allowed to settle into the grain of the paper. (Some heavy pigments never go into complete solution and when applied very wet they settle at the bottom of tiny puddles that form in the irregular surface of the paper.) In other places, as in the dark stroke indicating a wavelet in the extreme lower left corner, a relatively dry brushful of pigment has been dragged across the paper, leaving its grain showing as a speckling of white spots like flecks of foam or sparkles of light. Everywhere the paper tells; it is part of the technique. It tells in brilliance beneath the transparency of the pigment itself. It tells in passages like the sails or the side of the sloop, where it may even remain entirely unpainted or tinted with only the barest suggestion of color.

Water color thus applied has a freshness,

Figure 1

spontaneity, and clarity unique to itself. But the painter has no time to calculate or study, no opportunity to change or modify. Everything depends on his exact knowledge of what he is doing. He must work fast, against time, since ordinarily the paper must be damp during the process. The natural result of such speed is a style depending on suggestion rather than complete statement. Compare, for instance, the complications of Palmer's waterfall in *View of Tivoli* with the sweep of agitated water in *Sloop, Bermuda*, or the acute detail of the ruined temple with the broad suggestion of the boats and the men in them.

The hazard of a style like the one Homer used in this picture is that the painter may depend so much upon a standard bag of tricks that his water colors become sleight-of-hand performances rather than creative acts. This was not true of Homer; his water colors were incidental to his work in oil. It was in the oil technique, deliberate and thoughtful, that his art developed. His water colors emerge as brilliant summations of what he has learned in the oil technique. But the majority of painters who limit themselves to water color, no matter how technically expert they may be, fall into the trap of repetitious effects. The resultant anemic productions account for our idea that the technique is without substance.

To this unhappy generalization there are happy exceptions. For several good reasons John Marin is often called the greatest water-colorist who ever painted. For other major painters water color has always been the technique for studies, sketches, and minor works. Some have used it for the sheer pleasure of relaxation from more rigorous labors. But Marin is a water-colorist first of all; his oils reverse the usual order and seem to be efforts to adapt to a less compatible technique what he has learned about painting in water color. He used the unique advantages of water color to their fullest, forcing them, as in *The Singer Building*, to their very limit. He invested water color with a masculine force and used it with a creative originality unparalleled in its history.

It is easy to imagine Homer's *Sloop, Bermuda* translated into oil, even though it is a fine water color. It would be much changed in the process—compare it with Homer's most famous oil, *The Gulf Stream* (*Figure 2*), also a subject with water, a boat, and a figure—but the translation would be easy. On the other hand it is difficult to imagine Marin's *Boat off Deer Isle* (Plate 112) in any other technique than the one in which we see it, so completely are the expression and the means fused.

Boat off Deer Isle (its rather unwieldly full title is *Maine Series No. 9: Movement—Boat off Deer Isle*) is abstract and expressionistic, according to the principles discussed in the preceding portfolios on those subjects. It is not our purpose here to analyze it in those terms, and it must be assumed that the reader understands it from what has already been said. As an example of water-color painting *Boat off Deer Isle* is brilliant by any standard. The elements we have just mentioned in Homer's water color—the feel of the brush, the paper, and the water, the use of settling pigments, the revelation of paper texture by a dragged brush—all are present here but with a difference. In the Homer everything was directed toward suggesting the appearance of objects in brilliant outdoor light. In the Marin realistic

suggestion is no concern: the manipulation of water and pigment becomes in itself a form of expression, though not the only one, of course. Whereas Homer manipulates water color for description, Marin does so for expression, and that is why it is hardly possible to imagine *Boat off Deer Isle* in another technique. It is why Marin has a claim to the title of the finest and certainly the purest water-colorist of them all.

Marin's water colors offer the anomaly of an art combining spontaneity with a sense of complex and powerfully controlled organization, as we have seen in *The Singer Building*. It is also true in *Boat off Deer Isle*, which gives us an unusually strong clue to the way Marin composed a picture, combining on-the-spot decisions with a general predetermined scheme. On the left side there is a strong vertical line where, apparently, a puddle collected at the bottom of the heavy, blackish stroke and then, breaking, ran down the paper. It may certainly be taken for granted that this was an accident that, in any ordinary water color and in most Marins, would have been ruinous. In this particular picture, however, we may deduce that Marin saw the possibility of incorporating the line thus created into his general composition, countering or echoing it with the series of five similar black strokes at the right side of the picture and probably making adjustments in other elements that otherwise would not have had the same position or character. Admitting that the cultivation of such accidentals would hardly be a safe rule of procedure for Marin or for anybody else, it is still true that in this case the result was successful. It is an exaggerated illustration of the extraordinary unity between creative invention and the manipulation of a technique in Marin's art.

Pastel

Even more than water color, pastel is associated with ideas of the innocuous and the dainty. Pastel is one of the hundreds of varieties of colored crayons. Pigment combined with filler is pressed into stick form with enough gum to hold it together. This stick will vary in color intensity according to the proportion of pigment to the diluting filler; it varies in softness or hardness with the amount of gum. Since filler is less expensive than good pigment the average commercial pastel is pale, sometimes having the loveliness of "pastel shades" at their best, sometimes being merely weak and flat.

Pastel may be used on any surface with enough tooth to take the crayon under light pressure. A slick paper is no good at all. There are very fine sandpapers especially prepared for pastel, and it can also be used on fine-grained canvas. If pastel is to have any life at all the surface must have a grainy or powdery texture that accepts the pigment readily, even if this texture is close to microscopic. Beginners always overwork pastel, rubbing and smearing it to death. A skilled pastelist may rub a tone lightly here and there or even brush a whole area lightly, but not much. Every touch, once the pastel is applied, is dangerous; passages cannot be reworked because pastel is as unpleasant when overloaded with powder as when rubbed.

A completed pastel may be "fixed" with a light spray of diluted gum, but the fixative is only a help, not a real protection, to this most delicate of surfaces. If the fixative is applied heavily enough to hold the pastel firmly to the paper it will also spot it, deaden it, or give it an unpleasant shine. Pastels cannot be cleaned. If they are to endure they must be sealed under glass against all dust, dirt, and surface contacts.

Pastel enjoyed its liveliest vogue during the eighteenth century as a portrait medium. Its powdery, feminine tints were especially compatible with fashionable taste in decoration and costume; even the powdered coiffures of the period lent themselves to the chalkiness of

Figure 2

9

Figure 3

pastel description. The light touch, the intimacy, and the sensitive application of pastel harmonized beautifully with the light and graceful intention of the century's décor as well as its special kind of cultivated social personality. These same qualities have reduced the technique's popularity since then. It is used only sporadically in the work of most nineteenth- and twentieth-century painters. But it may occur with exceptional brilliance, as in a full-size detail from Édouard Manet's *George Moore* (Plate 113).

George Moore was a bright, clever, rather shallow young man, given over to superficialities of social intercourse rather than to great solidity or profundity of thought. It would not take much change to turn that description into a description of the pastel technique. Moore's coloring too, so very pale of skin and so pinkish-blond of hair and beard

10

that he was set apart from everybody else in a group, could have come straight out of a pastel box. With a subject perfectly suited to the technique Manet did one of the most wittily revealing portraits of his century, capitalizing to the full not only on the color and the delicacy of pastel but also on its capacity for quick suggestion. There are not many portraits that bring us so immediately and so freshly into the presence of the sitter, although there are a great many, including some by Manet, in which a more solid subject has given the painter opportunity to explore more significant nuances of personality and philosophy. But for these explorations painters have used the more solid technique of oil.

The great exception among pastelists is Edgar Degas. From what we have already said about him in other portfolios in discussing his *Woman with Chrysanthemums* (Plate 5, Portfolio 1) and *The Bellelli Family* (Plate 75, Portfolio 7), both oils, it is obvious that Degas is hardly in line with the pastel tradition of superficial delicacy or brilliance. His vigor, his precision, and his intellectualism are foreign to the generally innocuous run of pastels, nor was he content to turn to it as Manet did only for occasional use when a special subject could combine with the technique to produce an exceptional picture.

Still, pastel had certain advantages that Degas wanted to utilize. One of the greatest draughtsmen in the history of art, he was never altogether happy with oil paint. It is possible for a painter to draw with a brush, but a pencil or crayon is somehow a degree closer to the surface upon which he works. In pastel Degas experienced satisfaction as a draughtsman and became the only major painter to produce a large body of major works in the technique, giving it a strength and solidity hitherto foreign to it. This he did by building his pigment in successive layers. Ordinarily, as we have just said, such a way of working would have resulted in an unpleasant clotting of the pastel, if, indeed, it were possible at all, since there is

a limit to the amount of this powdery substance a surface can hold. Degas worked with a fixative prepared especially for him from a formula now unfortunately lost. With it, successive layers could be firmly fixed without loss of brilliance or the blemish of shine. Using crayons with a maximum of pigment and a minimum of filler, he avoided the obvious and limited effects of traditional pastel. His *The Toilet*, of which the entire picture (Plate 114) and a detail at full size (Plate 115) are reproduced in color, is the kind of picture in which Degas lifted pastel from its limbo of airy effects and sporadic brilliance to a firm place among the major techniques. An examination of the full-size detail should show how he juxtaposes one color at full intensity next to another to enhance the strength of both; how he drags one color across another so their intermixture vibrates with light. Forms emerge with a fullness and richness, rather than with the usual diaphanous suggestion of pastel.

Print Techniques: The Woodblock

Although several picturemaking processes had their origin as printed substitutes for drawings or paintings, they have grown into art forms in their own right. The simplest of these in principle, although not necessarily in execution, is the woodcut, which came into wide use in Europe in the Middle Ages as a means of reproducing illustrations for books.

A drawing was first made in black ink on a smooth piece of hard wood; then the uninked areas were cut away, leaving the drawing standing in relief, rubber-stamp fashion. Inked and printed, the block now gave, in reverse, a reproduction of a drawing that was more or less accurate according to the skill of the craftsman who cut it. Certain characteristics of the drawing had to be sacrificed, of course. Even the most accurate cutting could not entirely capture the freedom of the original

11

Figure 4

drawing. Gradations of tone were eliminated, as the value of the woodblock was that it could be quickly and uniformly inked and printed. On the other hand, since the denseness and uniformity of the printed line and its feeling of rigidity had their own attractiveness, artists doing work intended for woodcut reproduction learned to take these qualities into consideration in the original drawing.

A few artists cut their own blocks, but most of them were content to put the drawing on the wood and leave the cutting to craftsmen who specialized in this work. The cutting of a block requires considerable craftsmanship in itself. It is easy to draw a series of black lines on a piece of smooth wood, but it is not so easy to excise the areas between them.

Dürer's *Saint Christopher*, reproduced here at almost full size (*Figure 3*), is a woodcut. It could never quite be mistaken for a drawing, even though in modern printing it loses the slight variation in relief noticeable in the original where the block bites into the paper.

The general term "woodblock" includes woodcuts, as we have just described them, and wood engravings. William Blake's illustration for Thornton's Virgil, a tiny gem of a wood engraving, is also reproduced at exact size (*Figure 4*). Here the surface of the block was first painted over entirely in black and the cutting then done to reveal the drawing in whites. The difference takes a moment to grasp and may not seem important—but it is. The woodcut is conceived in blacks against whites, the wood engraving in whites against blacks. This distinction between woodcuts and

wood engravings is about as close as we can get without making dozens of reservations. Unfortunately this distinction doesn't hold even with the reservations when we get to recent work. A wood engraving is usually executed in very small, precise gouges and lines; a high degree of precision is implied. A modern print like Erich Heckel's illustration for a scene from Dostoevski (*Figure 5*) is obviously conceived in whites gouged out of blacks, but because they are gouged so vigorously, almost crudely, it is not by usual definition a wood engraving. We must be content to allow a generous leeway in these definitions, especially since the modern artist experiments with woodblocks in new directions every day.

The modern artist no longer regards the woodblock or any of the other print processes we are about to examine as a substitute for drawing. They are techniques with their own quality, just as oil, fresco, and water color are; the technique must be respected and its full potential exploited. The print processes have the advantage that large numbers of the same picture may be produced, but there are artists who would still work in prints even if it were possible to make only a single impression of each one.

In the scene from Dostoevski, Heckel has insisted upon what can only be called the "woodiness" of the block and has capitalized on its gouged quality just as a water-colorist might capitalize upon flow and transparency or as a painter in oil might take advantage of glazing, scumbling, and all the other potentials of that technique. The pioneer in this contemporary attitude toward the woodblock was Paul Gauguin. Working in Tahiti, he admired the accidental irregularities of batiks and stamped tapa cloths, where the natives' primitive technical processes left their mark so strongly on the finished product. He carried this idea into his woodcuts, frequently working on planks so rough that the grain reproduces in the printing. Instead of inking his blocks smoothly and printing them with uniform

12

pressure, he allowed (or even cultivated) the kind of irregularities that printmakers before him would have regarded as defects. He was not always successful; some of his prints are blurred and smeared to the point of being indecipherable. But in many, as in *Manao Tupapao*, or *The Spirit Watches* (Plate 116), these crudities are, by a sophisticated standard, appropriate to the primitivism of the subject. Certainly they bring us into the presence of the artist just as a painting does and as a technically perfect woodcut does not. We are close to him as he works, much closer than we

are in woodblocks in which the artist has drawn on the surface and then left the job of cutting to an intermediary technician.

Color Woodblock Prints

Before commenting further on *Manao Tupapao* we should examine some traditional color woodcuts. *Saint Christopher and Saint John the Baptist* (Plate 117) is a page from a book printed with wooden type and woodcut illustrations. (The inscription in the upper left corner is handwritten.) Then as a further

The Metropolitan Museum of Art

Figure 5

embellishment the illustrations were tinted by hand—rather crudely since this handwork took time and tended to cancel out the advantages of printing. In these early printed books there is a wonderful unity between type and illustration, since both were cut by hand from wood and thus shared an identity that is lost in a great deal of modern bookmaking where the type has one personality and the illustration is simply incorporated into the page without any regard for the harmony of the page as a whole. And even the relatively crude hand tinting has a vigor and directness in keeping with the whole. A delicately and meticulously tinted picture would be out of harmony—although this was not the consideration in mind when some apprentice was given the job of filling in certain areas with color.

The next step in the use of color was to make additional blocks from which the color areas could be printed. The Chinese and Japanese seem to have arrived independently and at about the same time at the idea of woodblock printing as a means of approximating drawings and paintings for multiple reproduction. An early Chinese print *Two Peaches on a Branch* (Plate 118) reproduces a water color after the artist Ko Chung-hsüan. The imitation of classical Chinese water-color style is successful enough to be completely deceptive at first glance. The shading on the gray branches and the blending of the pink tip of one peach into its yellow body are especially convincing. There is considerable speculation but no certain knowledge as to exactly how these gradations were created on the block, as we know they were, before the block was pressed onto moistened paper. The deep green leaves with dark veins are not quite so successful imitations of the quick manipulation of the painter's brush, but the accented outlines of the peaches, which not only thicken but also darken here and there, are so brushlike that they deny their print quality, as the craftsman meant them to do.

In the two early Japanese prints in Portfolio 5 (Plates 53 and 54) the block was cut to echo the shapes of brush strokes, but the printer makes no other attempt to capture brush character. Whereas *Two Peaches on a Branch* is still more painting than print, these two examples are already more print than painting. Before long the Japanese print flourished to the point where its merits as a print superseded its attractions as a pseudo painting.

During the eighteenth century the Japanese print crystallized into the exquisite form in which we know it best. A typical example is Harunobu's *Mother and Child with Bird* (Plate 119), reproduced here at about full size. In one small spot, where a pink flush spreads across the body of the little bird, graduated color is used, but elsewhere the colors are kept flat within marvelously precise linear definitions. Each color represents an individual block, cut with incredible nicety to register with the other color blocks within the framework of the black one that establishes the drawing and is called the "key block." Again, it is impossible to reproduce here the noticeable depressions along these hair-thin outlines that add so much life and definition to the original. Patterns are stamped into the paper here and there. In the mounds of white blossoms on the bush, detail is picked out in relief and within the gray pattern on the curtain to the right a secondary design is incised. There are also stamped patterns on the robes of the mother and the child. All these markings are apparent in the black and white detail taken in a raking light (*Figure 6*). This "blind printing," for which the French term *gaufrage* is frequently used, is done by a separate, uninked block. This expression of the cut block itself is the most dramatic demonstration of work conceived as a print, but everywhere the feeling is of color stamped, rather than washed, onto the paper.

It is characteristic of traditional Japanese art that it depends upon an almost fantastically developed craftsmanship, and it is characteristic of modern art that craftsmanship is sacrificed to individual expression. That is one

Figure 6

Figure 7

strong reason why Harunobu's *Mother and Child with Bird* and Gauguin's *Manao Tupapao* look so very different, although we are about to say that they are alike in their authenticity as prints. Technically they are at opposite poles, but the full enjoyment of each depends upon our recognition of the uses to which the artist has put his technique.

In different good impressions of the same Japanese print there will be certain minor differences, since the process is, after all, not a mechanical one but a hand one. But these differences are nothing at all compared with those in prints by Gauguin, which are so great that each print is virtually independent of others from the same blocks. Instead of applying his color uniformly over a defined area Gauguin may smear or rub it over an area or part of an area in any way he thinks may be most effective, and these differences and irregularities are exaggerated by the varying

pressures of unsystematic printing. *Manao Tupapao* is Gauguin's rarest print. At an early stage he ruined the block in making some additional cuttings, and only five impressions are known. Each of the five impressions has wide variations from the others, but in all of them the block and the process of creation is vividly, immediately present.

We may conjecture that Harunobu would have found *Manao Tupapao* unpardonably brutal, and so, in truth, Gauguin's prints seemed to most of his contemporaries. The tradition of Japanese draftsmanship is dominated by highly stylized line; in *Mother and Child with Bird*, as an instance, each line is beautiful in itself quite aside from its descriptive function, and each line is incorporated into a flow of rhythms that in its turn defines the integrated pattern of silhouettes. Yet if we look for these same characteristics in *Manao Tupapao* we can find them. The line and pat-

16

tern are more obvious and more direct, vigorous rather than exquisitely subtle, but ultimately they were fathered by Japanese prints, which Gauguin knew and admired and which influenced him without serving as models for imitation.

To conclude this discussion of woodblock prints we must return to *Manao Tupapao* to say that here and there Gauguin has added some spots of color with a brush. This practice horrifies printmakers but it can be defended here. The artist is not touching up a mistake but simply carrying on the creative process of a picture that he thinks of in terms as individual as those involved in the conception of a painting. He creates as he goes, rather than observing the mechanical niceties involved in reproducing uniformly a predetermined pattern. There is no such term as a woodblock-painting, but it could be coined to describe work like Gauguin's, not because he has actually painted into his print, but because the creative process continues and develops during the production of the print, just as it does in painting on canvas. He is, in a way, painting by means of a woodblock instead of a brush. Have we, then, come full circle back to *Two Peaches on a Branch*, which imitated painting? No, not at all. For this reason: whereas the craftsman who cut and printed *Two Peaches on a Branch* was imitating another technique, Gauguin's whole conception is stated in terms of the technique in which he is working.

Engraving

Printing is ordinarily thought of in the terms we have been describing—the inking and stamping of surfaces in relief. But it is also possible to print by the reverse of this method, by the intaglio process, in which the drawing is incised into the surface instead of raised above it. This is the process in metal plate engraving and in etching.

In engraving, once the picture has been cut into the metal plate in very fine, sharp, shallow

lines, the entire plate is thoroughly inked, with care taken that the ink is forced down into all of the lines, completely filling them. Then the surface is wiped clean, leaving the incised lines filled. If a piece of paper is laid over the plate and the plate and paper are run through a press operating on the old-fashioned clothes-wringer idea, the paper is pressed into each

Figure 8

MELENCOLIA I

Figure 9

18

line and picks up ink from it. The drawing is thus transferred to the paper, and the plate may be re-inked and used until it wears out. Since the face of the paper is forced into the cut lines, each line is reproduced not only in black ink but in the form of a very slight ridge. This is the texture we feel when we run our fingertips over an engraved invitation or calling card and explains the particular character of engraved line. Properly cut and properly printed, the engraved line has a razor-sharp definition and a brilliance beyond anything that can be achieved by pen line or a line printed by relief process.

One of the finest of all engravings is Pollaiuolo's *Battle of the Naked Men* (Figure 7). The reader may be weary of being reminded that in reproduction the various print processes lose some of their character. But it is important to remember, because so much of the enjoyment of prints comes from an under-

standing of the way the artist has used the technique. The severity of Pollaiuolo's style in *The Battle of the Naked Men*, his passion for exact definition of anatomical contours, and the masculine force of his design are all heightened by the tremendous discipline of the burin, the pointed cutting tool used by engravers. In this great print Pollaiuolo reaches a maximum expression of the controlled ferocity that characterizes his art. Something of the same nature is found in his *Martyrdom of Saint Sebastian* (Plate 65, Portfolio 6), in a typical combination with ornamental elegance that makes no concessions to prettiness or even to grace. The friezelike background of *The Battle of the Naked Men* reflects Pollaiuolo's training in the demanding craft of goldsmithery, one that must have contributed a great deal to his exceptional skill as an engraver. *The Battle of the Naked Men* is the only engraving known to be by Pollaiuolo, but

Figure 10

Figure 11

19

Figure 12

Figure 13

alone it places him high in the hierarchy of that art. No other engraving surpasses this one in the complete unity between technique and image.

The engraver's burin is a sharp triangular gouge that cuts cleanly into the metal plate, excising with great precision the tiny channel that becomes in printing a sharp black ridge of a line. The depth and width of the burined line depends upon the degree of pressure the craftsman applies in the cutting. A skillful engraver can accent a line by thickening it or thinning it, but the range is narrow, limited by the capacity to print sharply. This "shaded line" has the sparkle and contrast of all engraved lines plus a suggestion of flexibility.

In a detail at actual size (*Figure 8*) from *The Battle of the Naked Men* it should be apparent that each line is produced with absolute control and that any slip throwing a single line or portion of a line out of relation to the others would have been fatal. The metal plate, engraved and ready for inking, is in itself a beautiful thing. Each line glistens with the

same quality as engraved initials on silverware, which of course are produced in the same way. Theoretically it would be possible to reproduce (always in reverse) the initials from ordinary tableware by filling them with ink in the way described and pressing paper into them. The art of pictorial engraving probably originated in some such way when the engravers of ornamental designs on armor or other decorated metal took impressions of their patterns in this way and thus recorded them for future reference.

Limited as he is to thin lines, the engraver who wants to produce varieties of gray tones must do so by a multitude of crisscrossings, or a series of straight lines close together, or a stippling of tiny short strokes or dots, as Albrecht Dürer has done in another masterpiece, his great *Melancholia I*. The entire engraving is reproduced here close to full size (*Figure 9*), with enlargements of two areas that show how the different textures and tonalities were produced by different combinations of the burin line (*Figures 10 and 11*).

20

Etching

The extreme discipline of cutting a drawing into a metal plate rules out the quick, sketchy line of free drawing. This restriction is removed in another intaglio process, etching. The plate is similarly inked, wiped, and printed, but the line is produced in another way.

To make an etching the artist first covers a metal plate (usually of copper) with a wax coating called "ground," which is impervious to acid. With a fine stylus point he can draw on this ground with all the freedom of pen or pencil. The sharp point removes the wax where he draws, exposing the metal to the action of an acid bath that "bites" into the surface of the plate. The artist controls the width of the line by the depth of biting. Heavy lines are produced by longer exposure to the acid. Lighter ones are "stopped out" midway by removing the plate from the bath and painting that area with the impervious ground.

An etched line is entirely different in character from an engraved one. It is softer, warmer, richer. Whereas the burin cuts precisely, the acid eats out a little chasm with uneven edges. Rembrandt's *Christ Carried to the Tomb* (*Figure 12*) and an enlargement (*Figure 13*) can be compared with *The Battle of the Naked Men* and *Melancholia* to show the resultant difference after printing.

An engraved plate is always inked and wiped with maximum care to produce as sharp and brilliant an image as possible, since these are the characteristic virtues of the technique. So are some etchings, but since an etched line is ordinarily softer than an engraved one, some etchers increase the effect of softness by not wiping the plate quite clean. A little film of ink may be left where a tone is desired over

Figure 14

Figure 15

a certain passage. Rembrandt, among others, utilized this trick of wiping, but Whistler, at the end of the nineteenth century, used it to an unprecedented extent. In an etching like his *Nocturne* (*Figure 14*) the actual etched passages are limited to a few lines suggesting a ship and distant architecture. The light on the horizon, the darkening sky, and its reflection in the lagoon are all produced by wiping. In the history of etching Whistler's revolution was not as great as Gauguin's in woodblock printing, but it still had a tremendous impact.

Aquatints

Tones from pale gray to rich black can be bitten into a metal plate by the aquatint process. In this technique, the plate is dusted very thinly with powdered rosin. When the plate is heated from the under side the microscopic granules melt and adhere to its surface.

Like regular etching ground they are impervious to acid, so when the plate is put into the bath the acid eats into the metal only in the tiny interstices between the granules and only, of course, in areas that have not been blocked off in preparing the design of the print. The texture and darkness are controlled by the amount of dusting and the time of exposure to acid. Goya's *Old Man among Ghosts* (*Figure 15*) was toned with aquatint after the drawing was completely bitten in. An enlarged portion brings us closer to the texture (*Figure 16*).

Dry Point

Dry point is an intaglio process related to etching and engraving, a technique in which the drawing is scratched directly into the metal plate with a stylus, without benefit of biting acids. (An etching may be touched up by such gouged lines—but always with the danger that

22

its different character may not be in harmony with the etched lines.) A line gouged with a stylus is different from one cut with a burin. The burin completely excises the thread of metal from the body of the plate, but the stylus may throw it up unevenly on either side of the gouge, like earth from a plow. When the plate is inked these "plowed up" edges hold additional ink that, under the pressure of printing, squeezes out in a soft or even fuzzy addition to the line. The effect of dry point may be one of great richness. But very fine, delicate lines may also be produced in dry point by polishing away the ragged edge. Enlarged dry-point lines are shown here (*Figure 17*).

Lithography

Finally, a third print classification besides relief and intaglio processes is the planographic one. A lithograph prints from neither raised nor depressed lines but from a flat surface by utilizing the simple principle of the incompatibility of oil and water. A lithograph is drawn with a black grease crayon on a slab of smooth, fine grained stone. The stone's surface is then treated with a preparation that makes the stone itself repellent to grease except where it has been touched with the black (lithographic) crayon. But every place the stone has been so touched it is ready to accept grease. When a roller covered with lithographic ink, which has an oil or grease base, is run over the surface, the drawing becomes inked and ready for printing, with virtually no loss of detail.

After a sheet of paper is placed on this surface, the stone and paper are run through a press that exerts a scraping pressure, and the drawing is transferred (reversed) from stone to paper. The process can be repeated until the image breaks down from wear.

Kathe Kollwitz's *The Summons of Death*

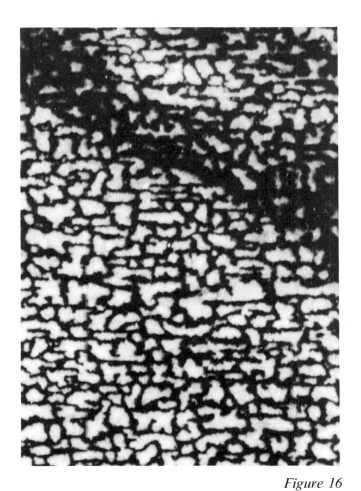

Figure 16

Figure 17

23

Figure 18

(*Figure 18*) could be mistaken for a crayon drawing as neither engravings nor etchings would be mistaken for pen or pencil; in lithographs we are particularly close to the artist as a draughtsman.

As is apparent in *The Summons of Death*, lithography affords the entire range from the darkest, richest blacks to the pure white of the paper. The distinctive grainy quality of the grays comes from the texture of the stone. In the Kollwitz lithograph the drawing is exceptionally vigorous and direct. The lithographic crayon is square in section—about one fourth of an inch—and in the broad strokes at the left the various gradations within single strokes are made by varying pressure. A stroke beginning wide and ending thin and graduated from light to dark, like several in this example, is made in a single, sure motion of the hand, not only by varying pressure but by turning the crayon to a different angle as it is pulled across the stone. At the opposite pole there are the delicate, tenuous lines of the hand coming into the picture from the right.

Color lithography is a rich field for the printmaker, coming closer than any other technique to the variety and flexibility of painting. Toulouse-Lautrec's *Clown* (Plate 120) involves color as well as half a dozen different methods of applying the crayon, including its liquid form, which is called "tusche." In color lithography a different stone is prepared for each color, just as in woodblock printing. These are printed in sequence over one another. In woodblock printing two colors are sometimes printed over one another to produce a third—blue over yellow to produce a green, for instance—but the result is likely to be a little thick and heavy. In lithography, however, the grainy texture of the stone, with its peppering of tiny clear areas throughout, is wonderfully receptive to overprinting. The undercolor shows through the open spaces of the overcolor and gives an additional vibrancy to the resultant color as its two elements play against one another.

In *Clown* the ruff, or collar, was painted on the stone with a soft brush and liquid crayon, and the spots on the floor were apparently dabbed in with the end of a stiffer brush, less heavily loaded with tusche. The speckling over the entire stone was made by holding a stiff brush well above its surface and scraping the bristles against some rigid edge or possibly by flipping them lightly with the thumb. This spattering was built up within certain definite areas—as the bench and the wall back of the head—by protecting the rest of the stone with pieces of paper laid over it, stencil fashion.

Toulouse-Lautrec's departure from conventional lithographic techniques corresponds to Gauguin's in the woodblock and is at least as important in the history of printmaking. Like Gauguin he enlarged the scope of a print technique to the point where it became an art form in its own right.

The print processes we have described are the basic ones. There have been many variations on them in the past; there are countless ones today. Etching, lithography, engraving, and woodcut may all be combined in a single print; inks may be applied in new ways to create unexpected textures; pigment may be built up into high relief. Many prints are unclassifiable into conventional groups, and "combined media" is a blanket term now used to cover them.

Any museum, no matter how small, can afford to own good prints, and the amateur who collects art, no matter on how modest a scale, is no subject to the murderous competition that makes paintings so expensive. He may never own an impression of *The Battle of the Naked Men* or *Melancholia*, but he can develop an eye for the best of the current production and may have for a few dollars some first-rate prints. And he owns originals. He also owns works of art that are not imitations of or substitutes for reproductions of paintings. He owns woodblock prints, engravings, etchings, and lithographs conceived as works of art in their own right.

Notes on the Artists

Albrecht Dürer, 1471-1528, German

109. MADONNA AND CHILD WITH A MULTITUDE OF ANIMALS, ABOUT 1503

Pen and water color. Height 12⅝". The Albertina, Vienna

Albrecht Dürer was a painter, an engraver, and a maker of woodcuts; he is represented in all three capacities in this portfolio. Generally acknowledged as the greatest of all German painters, he was also one of the greatest painters of his time and for that matter of all time. His technical gifts were staggering; his engravings alone are enough to establish him as a master. His intellectual power and his moral force are as great as his technical genius, although less apparent in the charming tinted drawing *Madonna and Child with a Multitude of Animals* than in his engravings. Among these *Melancholia I (Figure 9)* is supreme.

Melancholia is one of a trio of engravings, one of which, *Knight, Death, and the Devil*, is an allegory of man's journey through life beset by the forces of evil, while another, *Saint Jerome in His Study*, is a serene and warming tribute to the life of contemplation and intellectual satisfaction away from the hurly-burly of daily life. *Melancholia*, on the other hand, is a philosophical statement about man's nature and a question about the significance of his presence in the world. Beyond an allegorical female figure sitting in the midst of symbols of erudition and the arts stretches an infinite sea beneath a sky where comets blaze. Yet here at the center of the universe, the figure surrounded by the accumulated learning of the ages is distressed and full of doubts; she seems to question the end toward which man's achievements have been directed, if indeed they have been directed toward any goal at all in the immensity of time and the world. It was this spirit of doubt that was to shatter the enthusiastic period of discovery that was the early Renaissance. *Melancholia* has been called a prophecy of the dilemma of modern man. A century later Shakespeare would extend the doubt and pessimism of *Melancholia* in a more bitter comment when Macbeth finds life a "tale told by an idiot, full of sound and fury, signifying nothing."

Madonna and Child with a Multitude of Animals, with its appropriate gentleness and sweetness, is another matter. But Dürer's probing mind is not at rest even here. With the renaissance man's passionate curiosity to learn the secrets of the world he has drawn each animal and each plant with a detailed realism that is not imitation of surface appearance but a near-scientific analysis of each form, as a botanist or a zoologist might examine them. Here he combines renaissance investigation with medieval mysticism, for each of these animals and each of these plants is at the same time part of a world united in the adoration of the Madonna.

Samuel Palmer, 1805-1871, British

110. VIEW OF TIVOLI, ABOUT 1838

Pencil, water color, and gouache. Height 12⅞". The Philadelphia Museum of Art

Samuel Palmer was a child prodigy who had three landscape drawings in the exhibition of the Royal Academy when he was only fourteen years old. He was always of an imaginative turn of mind, but it was not until he met William Blake that he began to trust his own love for creating poetically visionary subjects. His most individual paintings are romantic, moonlit landscapes where ordinary countryside scenes, frequently with grazing sheep, take on a supernatural quality in mysterious illumination. The exact date of *View of Tivoli* is not known, but presumably it was done at the time of his marriage and Italian honeymoon. Although it is not typical of the moonlit scenes just mentioned, it is highly romanticized. Even granted that scenes around Tivoli are romantic in themselves, he has made the most of the darkening recesses between hills, the spreading light at the horizon, and the small figures harmonized with the deep space of nature. All this is a particularly English conception of landscape. Palmer is a minor master in the school; many have excelled him in expressing the grandeur of nature, but no one has excelled him in intimate sensitivity.

Winslow Homer, 1836-1910, American

111. SLOOP, BERMUDA, 1899

Water color. Height 15". The Metropolitan Museum of Art, Lazarus Fund, 1910

Winslow Homer is usually thought of as one of the two painters who were most typically American in the nineteenth-century period when the most successful painters were imitating European manners. The other, Thomas Eakins, has also been seen in this series (Plate 22, Portfolio 2). Both men painted Americans and the American scene in a straightforward fashion, with an honesty and a solidity we like to think of as typically American. Homer began as an illustrator, especially for *Harper's Weekly*; his assignments for that publication included a coverage of the Civil War. When he began painting he found his subject matter in New England farm life and the life of the fishermen on the New England coast. During this time he did water colors as well as oils, but in a tight, detailed style. *Sloop, Bermuda* is from his later period when, under the influence of English water-colorists, he adopted the bold, free, economical style described in the text. Although Homer suffered no financial hardship, his success during his lifetime was relatively modest, at least in comparison with the very high place he now occupies in American art. He seemed too simple, not as high-flown or "arty" as the academic painters who were commanding the best prices from a fashionable market. Of course it is this very simplicity, a native vigor, that is appreciated in his art today, while the artiness of the academic painters has relegated them to museum basements.

John Marin, 1870-1953, American

112. BOAT OFF DEER ISLE, 1926

Water color. Height 15⅞". The Philadelphia Museum of Art

John Marin, who has already been discussed in Portfolio 3, was of French ancestry and spent six years in France as a young man. There are, however, certain qualities that make him distinctly an American painter of the international school of the twentieth century. It is not so much that he found his subjects in the great bridges and skyscrapers of American cities and the rugged coasts of Maine as that his work is full of the clangor and virility of the first and the rugged vigor of the other. He sees and feels as a participator in the American experience, rather than as a fascinated observer of it, as most European painters have been who essayed American subjects.

Historically Marin is an important figure in the initiation of the American public into the mysteries of modern art. When the photographer Alfred Stieglitz opened his art gallery "291" in New York in 1905 Marin was one of the vanguard painters represented there. From that time on he was consistently an important figure in the organization of *avant-garde* exhibitions of high caliber, avoiding the "band wagonism" that later marred so much of the missionary work for the modern art cause. Unlike very many other pioneers, he received generous recognition during his lifetime, with important exhibitions here and in Europe, including one at the great international Biennial Exhibition of 1950 in Venice, where two rooms were devoted to his work.

Édouard Manet, 1832-1883, French

113. Detail from GEORGE MOORE, ABOUT 1879

Pastel. Height of detail 11⅞". The Metropolitan Museum of Art, H. O. Havemeyer Collection, 1929

Manet has figured rather conspicuously in these portfolios (Plates 23, 107 in Portfolios 2, 9), and that is as it should be. His is one of the several legitimate claims to the title of father of modern art. In his case, it is a matter of his having established once and for all the painter's right to paint as he pleased and to be judged on his own merits rather than by a formula set up by a group of painters in positions of entrenched privilege. Although it is difficult to see how his work could have been considered shocking, it was exhibited only in the face of scandal and abuse.

George Moore, the subject of the portrait in this portfolio, was a young Irishman who had come to Paris to study under Cabanel, one of the most conventional of the conventional painters who opposed Manet. But Moore's taste was not much for hard work, and he soon discovered that nights at the cafés and along the boulevards were much more attractive than days in the studio. At the Café de la Nouvelle Athènes, a gathering place for Manet and his friends, he listened to the discussions of painters and writers and became an ardent francophile. He abandoned his own efforts to paint. Turned essayist and novelist, he later became a mildly leavening influence on English literature. At his best he was a graceful stylist, at his worst a poseur guilty of pretentious persiflage. Manet did other drawings of him, always with the same acute perspicacity that marks the pastel of our illustration. One wonders if Moore realized how nakedly his nature was revealed in them.

Hilaire Germain Edgar Degas, 1834-1917, French

114. THE TOILET, ABOUT 1885

> Pastel. Height 29⅛". The Metropolitan Museum of Art, H. O. Havemeyer Collection, 1929

115. Detail from THE TOILET

In the previous examples of Degas's art, *Woman with Chrysanthemums* (Plate 5, Portfolio 1) and the wonderful *Bellelli Family* (Plate 75, Portfolio 7), we discussed his psychological penetration and analyzed the means by which he relayed his observations through composition. *The Toilet* reveals another aspect of his art, a late one that has been unflatteringly tagged "keyhole art." And it is true that in his intimate scenes of women dressing or undressing, bathing, and drying themselves, he presents the nude in a new aspect, one in which the model is unaware of the observer. The self-display, the elaborate, graceful poses, and the beautification of the average painted nude presupposes an audience. Degas is not interested in idealization; his preoccupation is with the attitude casually and unconsciously assumed. Exactly as he caught the woman with chrysanthemums in a momentary gesture that makes her more alive and more present than she would have been if she had been formally posed, so he does with these intimate scenes in which the model is caught unaware. When he used a model, Degas never put her in a pose but had her move freely around the studio as he observed her. Later he would fabricate the figure from memory or from the briefest notations. This, of course, was in his late work; in early work he followed more conventional procedures. A supreme master of drawing, he created figures in which every bone and every bit of flesh is convincingly present without being represented in detail. In his old age his sight failed and he was forced to work in a broad, rather soft manner, but even in these works his mastery of form is complete, and with a few sketchy notations he could create a whole figure of convincing reality.

Paul Gauguin, 1848-1903, French

116. MANAO TUPAPAO, 1894

> Color woodcut retouched with water color. Height 8⅞". The Philadelphia Museum of Art

Paul Gauguin, who belonged to the generation of painters coming after Degas and revolting against the impressionism of which Degas was one of the great masters, was nevertheless a great admirer of Degas's art, as Degas was of Gauguin's. Degas in fact bought several paintings by the younger man for his own collection. Although they were so different in their approach, Gauguin being a symbolist and Degas a realist, both founded their art on the cultivation of line as the basic factor in the expression of form, and this was the source of their mutual admiration. *Manao Tupapao* was done during the last, terrible years of Gauguin's life when, sick and bankrupt, he was achieving his finest work in self-imposed exile from the studios of Paris, in the South Seas. Gauguin wanted to combine the savage simplicity of primitive art with a set of highly civilized theories of esthetics, a paradoxical combination that gives his art its special quality and one that does not always come off. In this woodcut the "crude" technique and the "awkwardness" of the forms are calculated as part of a composition that observes fairly conventional ideas of linear relationships and does manage to bring about a successful fusion of Gauguin's two contradictory ideals.

German School, XV century

117. SAINT CHRISTOPHER AND SAINT JOHN THE BAPTIST

Hand-colored woodcut. Height 9½". The Metropolitan Museum of Art, bequest of James C. McGuire, 1931

The process of multiplying a drawn image by printing it from a wooden block or a metal plate was a momentous development in the history of Western civilization. From that time pictures, heretofore owned by the privileged few, became an increasingly popular form of communication. The earliest printed pictures in Europe were probably made around 1400 or shortly after. These were woodcuts, principally sacred pictures and playing cards, often brightly and roughly colored by hand in the manner of the example we have reproduced.

After Ko Chung-hsüan, XVII century, Chinese

118. TWO PEACHES ON A BRANCH, ABOUT 1633

Color woodcut. Diameter 9¾". The Philadelphia Museum of Art

The Ten Bamboo Studio (*Shih-chu-chai Shu Hua P'u*, or Treatise on the Paintings and Writings of the Ten Bamboo Studio) is a set of books combining poems with pictures of flowers, fruits, birds, and stones. First appearing in the first third of the seventeenth century, it went into many subsequent editions of varying quality. Although there is much confusion on this score, the page reproduced in this portfolio appears to be from a first edition. The books are masterpieces of color printing by any standard. The intent was to approximate the characteristic look of oriental water color, and, as pointed out in the text, the craftsmen who reproduced original water colors in the form of woodblock prints achieved an amazingly close approximation.

Suzuki Harunobu, 1725-1770, Japanese

119. MOTHER AND CHILD WITH BIRD

Color woodcut. Height 10⅞". The Philadelphia Museum of Art

Suzuki Harunobu was one of the most poetic of the Japanese printmakers. The earliest Japanese prints, like the ones illustrated in Portfolio 5 (Plates 53 and 54), were of actors, courtesans, or other subjects having to do with the world of public gaiety and entertainment. Harunobu, on the other hand, developed the print as a means for representing intimate domestic scenes of the utmost delicacy. Instead of beautiful courtesans he delineated modest and well-bred young girls; instead of actors and dancers, mothers and children; instead of public places or famous scenic spots, the interiors of homes of good families and the secluded corners of their gardens, like the charming scene *Mother and Child with Bird*. Harunobu made great technical advances. Although the end effect of his prints is one of tenderness and simplicity, he used an unusually large number of colors, sometimes more than ten. But the subtle tonalities, including many light grays, retain the effect of simplicity that would have been lost had he been tempted to display his technical skill by making strong color differentiations. He was also particularly adept in the use of gaufrage, mentioned in the text. In spite of the technical complexity of his work he was enormously productive; between six and seven hundred prints are known to be from his hand.

Henri de Toulouse-Lautrec, 1864-1901, French

120. CLOWN, 1896

Color lithograph. Height 20⅝". The Metropolitan Museum of Art, Alfred Stieglitz Collection, 1949

Henri de Toulouse-Lautrec was discussed in Portfolio 5 in connection with his poster *Aristide Bruant* (Plate 60). Like that poster, the lithograph *Clown* shows one of the theatrical characters he delighted in representing, one of the dozens of clowns, actors, singers, dancers, acrobats, animal trainers, and musicians of the vivid but fleeting world through which he moved. Lautrec not only represented them as they performed, recording their faces, bodies, and costumes, but also—and more importantly—he has caught them as if unawares in moments of rest between performances. In *Clown* he has preserved with extraordinary brilliance a world that is ordinarily here for a moment and then vanished forever. The female clown Cha-U-Kao served Lautrec for a number of paintings and drawings in addition to his famous lithograph. She entertained at the Moulin Rouge and at the "New Circus" with a grotesque act including a certain amount of eccentric dancing and apparently some elementary animal training. Another of Lautrec's pictures, one of his most trenchant comments on the world he knew, is included in Portfolio 11 on the artist as a social critic.